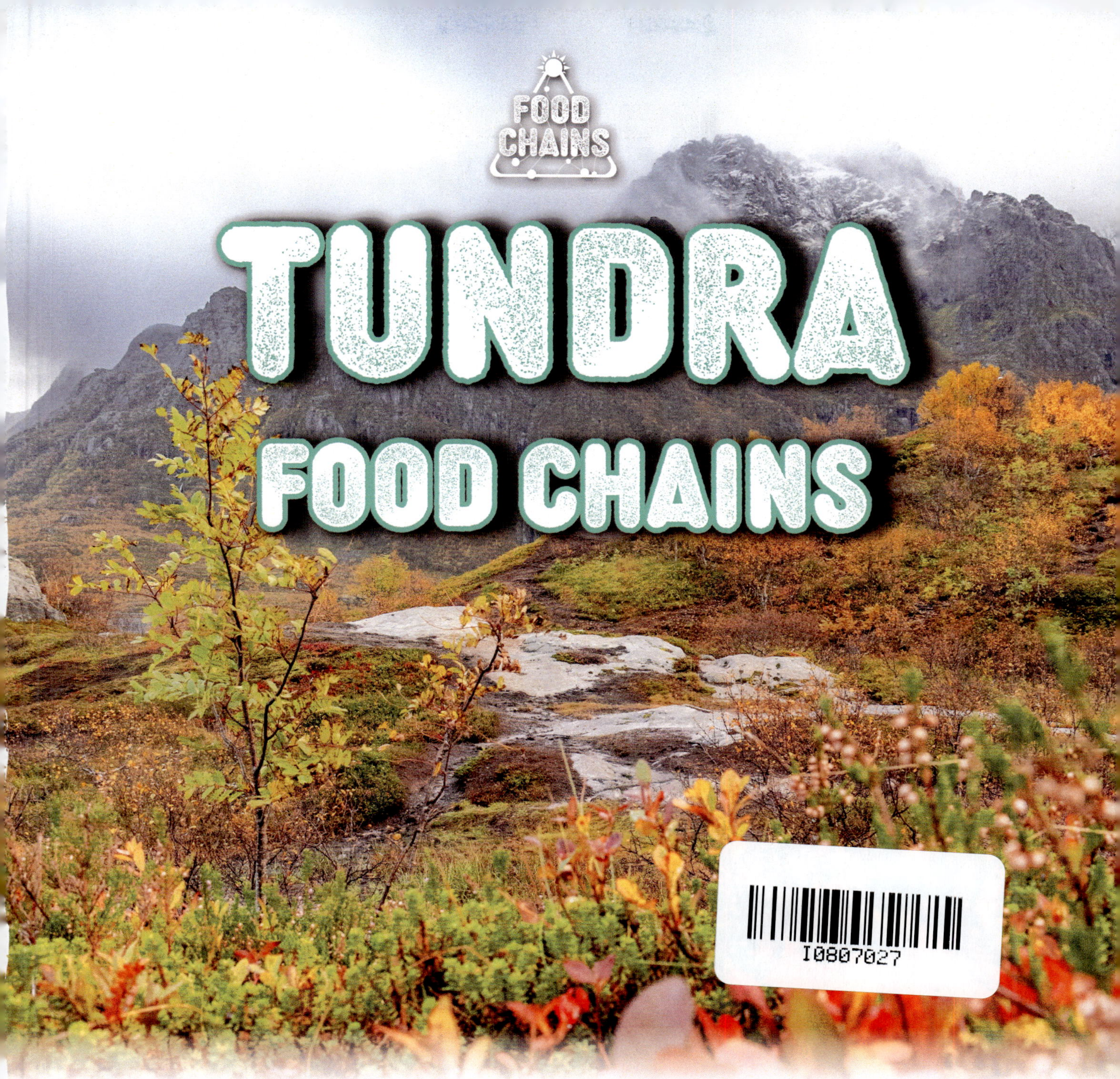

FOOD CHAINS

TUNDRA FOOD CHAINS

Kelley MacAulay and Bobbie Kalman

A Crabtree Crown Book

Crabtree Publishing
crabtreebooks.com

TUNDRA FOOD CHAINS

Created by Bobbie Kalman

Editor-in-chief
Bobbie Kalman

Writing team
Kelley MacAulay
Bobbie Kalman

Substantive editor
Kathryn Smithyman

Editors
Molly Aloian
Reagan Miller

Production manager
Candice Campbell

Design
Margaret Salter

Consultant
Patricia Loesche, Ph.D., Animal Behavior Program, Department of Psychology, University of Washington

Cover
Rhea Magaro-Wallace

Images
All images: Shutterstock.com

Crabtree Publishing

crabtreebooks.com 800-387-7650

In Canada: We acknowledge the financial support of the Government of Canada through the Canada Book Fund for our publishing activities.

Printed in the U.S.A./CP032026

Published in Canada
Crabtree Publishing
616 Welland Ave.
St. Catharines, Ontario
L2M 5V6

Published in the United States
Crabtree Publishing
347 Fifth Ave.
Suite 1402-145
New York, NY 10016

Library and Archives Canada Cataloguing in Publication
Available at the Library and Archives Canada

Library of Congress Cataloging-in-Publication Data
Available at the Library of Congress

Hardcover: 978-1-0398-7301-8
Paperback: 978-1-0398-7359-9
Ebook (pdf): 978-1-0398-7410-7
Epub: 978-1-0398-7459-6

CONTENTS

WHAT IS THE TUNDRA?

In winter, the tundra is covered with snow. Some animals, such as this arctic wolf, remain on the tundra even during freezing winters.

Many tundra animals, such as this spruce grouse hen, eat the plants that grow in summer.

The **tundra** is a large area of frozen land. It has almost no trees. The tundra circles the Earth in the far northern parts of North America, Europe, and Siberia. Just south of the tundra is another area that circles the Earth. It is called the **taiga**. The taiga is a forest made up of **coniferous** trees.

Extreme weather

Winter lasts almost the entire year on the tundra! Temperatures are usually only -32 °F (-36 °C), and **blizzards**, or snowstorms with strong winds, are common. For six to 10 weeks a year, the tundra warms up. Summer temperatures reach only 54 °F (12 °C), and rain almost never falls. The weather is warm enough for many kinds of plants to grow, however.

Always frozen

On the tundra, most of the ground remains frozen all year. Even in summer, temperatures are not warm enough to thaw the ground completely. Only the top 8 inches (20 cm) of ground thaws in summer. Under this top layer is a thick layer of frozen ground. This layer of the ground is called **permafrost** because it is permanently frozen. Water cannot sink into permafrost. The water stays in the soil, making the soil soggy.

In the dark

The tundra receives different amounts of sunlight at different times of the year. In winter, the sun may not rise for two months! In summer, the tundra may receive sunlight all day and all night for weeks at a time.

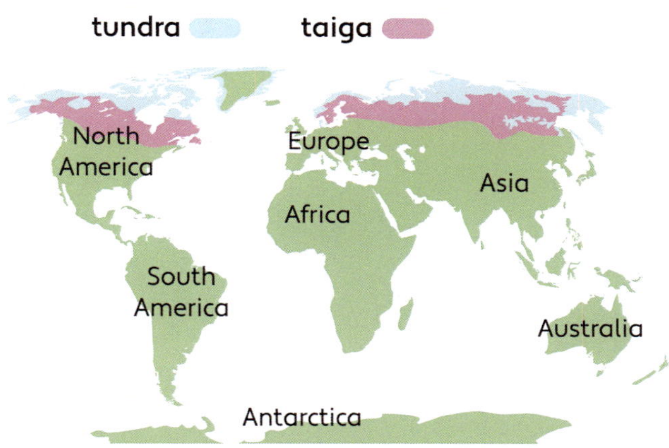

This polar bear is searching for food along the banks of an icy river on the tundra.

WHAT IS A FOOD CHAIN?

The tundra is home to certain plants and animals. Plants and animals are living things. All living things need water, sunlight, air, and food to stay alive. Plants and animals receive **nutrients** from food.

Nutrients are substances that plants and animals need to stay healthy. Plants and animals also get **energy** from food. Plants use energy to grow. Animals need energy to breathe air, to grow, and to move around.

These caribou are eating tundra plants to get nutrients and energy.

Food for plants

Plants and animals get food in different ways. Plants can **produce**, or make, their own food using energy from the sun! Plants are the only living things that can make their own food.

Food for animals

Animals must eat to get nutrients and energy from food. Different kinds of animals eat different foods. Some animals eat plants, and some eat other animals. Many animals eat both plants and animals. The pattern that is created when animals eat to get food energy is called a **food chain**. This book is about food chains found on the North American tundra. The diagram on the right explains how a food chain works.

Energy from the sun

Green plants trap some of the sun's energy and use it to make food. They use some of the energy as food and store the rest.

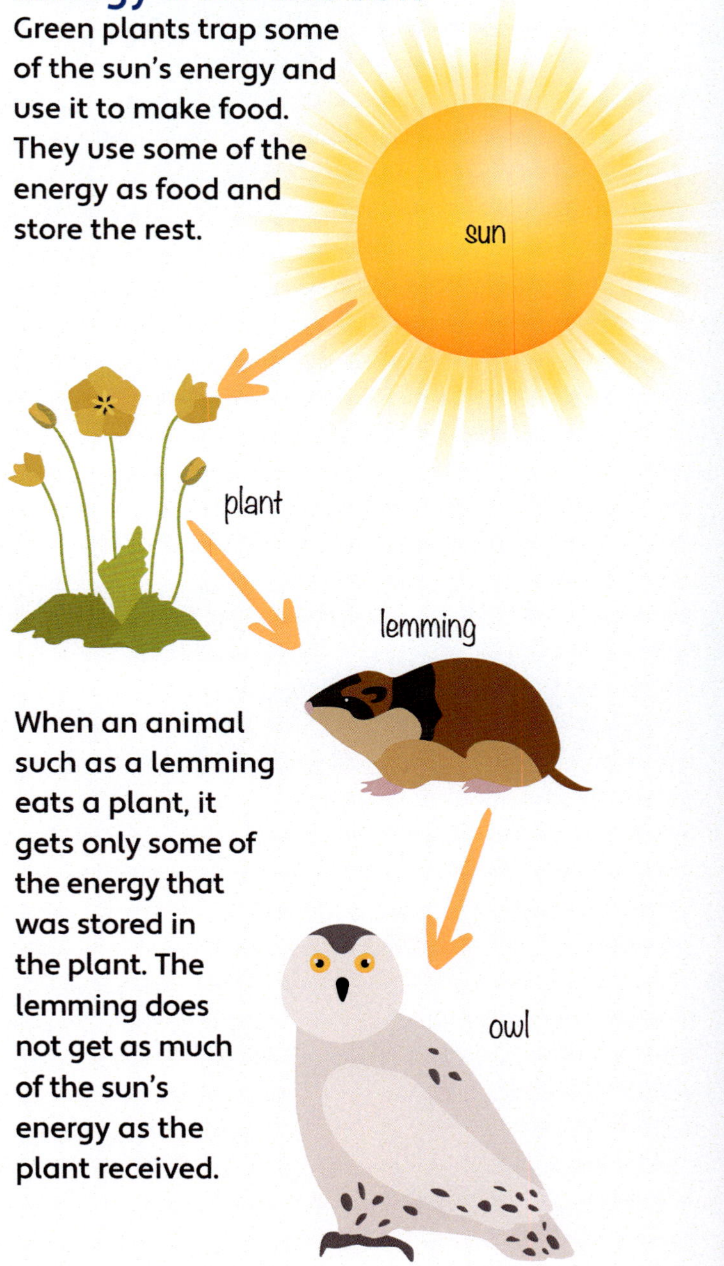

When an animal such as a lemming eats a plant, it gets only some of the energy that was stored in the plant. The lemming does not get as much of the sun's energy as the plant received.

When an owl eats a lemming, energy is passed to the owl through the lemming. The owl gets less of the sun's energy than the amount the lemming received.

FOOD CHAINS HAVE LEVELS

Each food chain has three levels. The first level is made up of plants. Animals that eat plants make up the second level. The third level is made up of animals that eat other animals.

Plants produce food

"**Primary**" means "first." Plants are the **primary producers** in food chains because food chains start with them. Plants do not use all the food they make. They store the food they do not use as energy.

Animals that eat plants

The second level of a food chain is made up of animals that eat plants. These animals are called **herbivores**. They are also called **primary consumers** because they are the first living things in a food chain that must **consume**, or eat, food to get energy. Herbivores receive some of the sun's energy that was stored in plants.

Animals that eat meat

Carnivores are animals that eat other animals. They make up the third level of food chains. Carnivores are **secondary consumers**—they are the second group of living things in a food chain that eat to get energy. When carnivores eat herbivores or other carnivores, they receive less of the sun's energy than the other animals received.

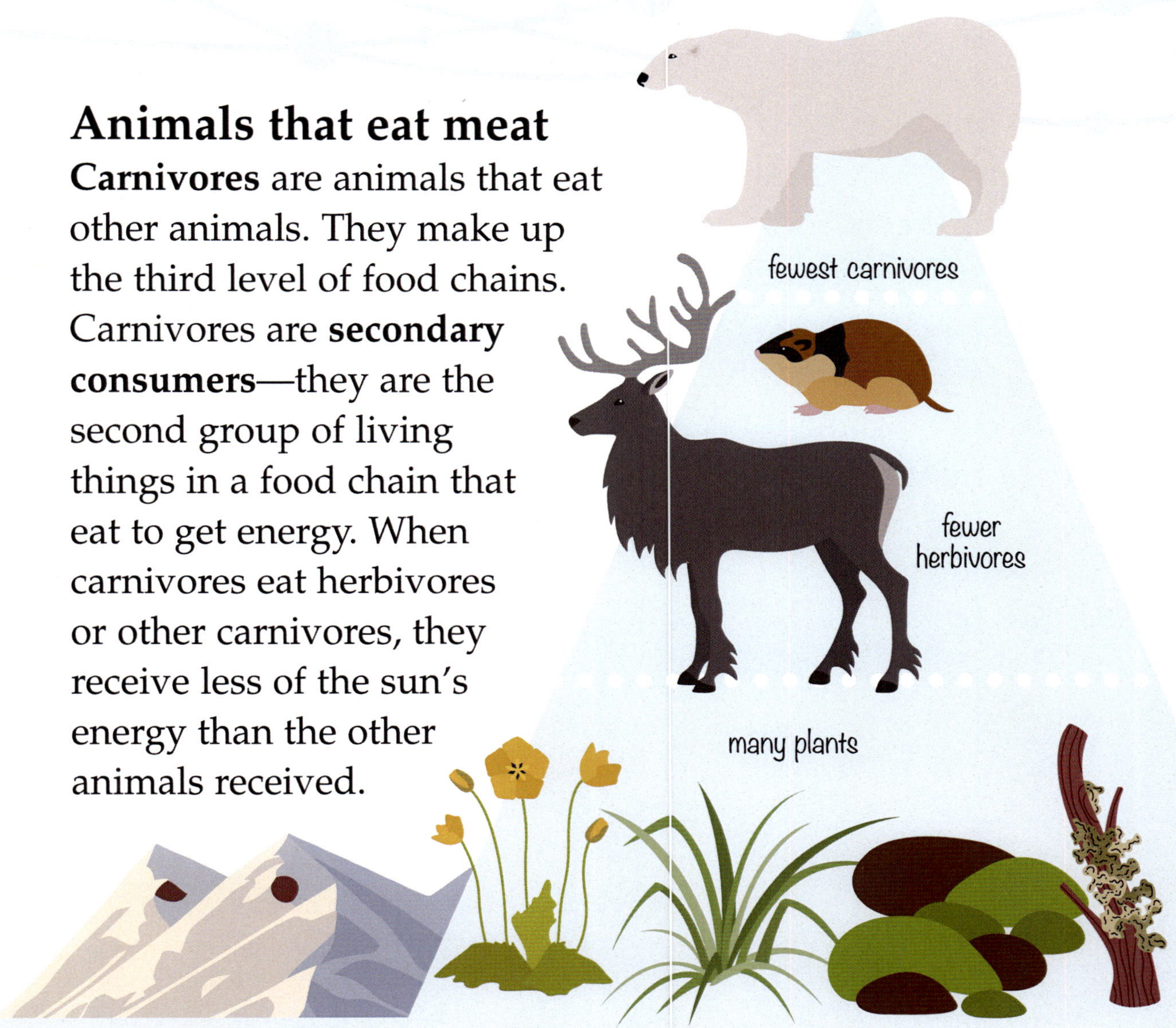

The energy pyramid

This **energy pyramid** shows the flow of energy in a food chain. A pyramid is wide at the bottom and narrow at the top. The energy pyramid is wide at the first level to show that there are many plants. It takes many plants to make enough food energy for animals. The pyramid's second level narrows because there are fewer herbivores than there are plants. There are fewer herbivores because each one must eat many plants. The top level of the pyramid is the narrowest because there are fewer carnivores than any other living things in a food chain. Each carnivore must eat many herbivores to get the food energy it needs.

PRODUCING FOOD

Plants produce food through a process called **photosynthesis**. Plants have a green **pigment**, or color, in their leaves called **chlorophyll**. Chlorophyll has two jobs. First, it takes in energy from the sun.

Second, chlorophyll combines the sun's energy with water, nutrients from the soil, and with **carbon dioxide**, a gas found in air. The food a plant makes is called **glucose**, which is a type of sugar.

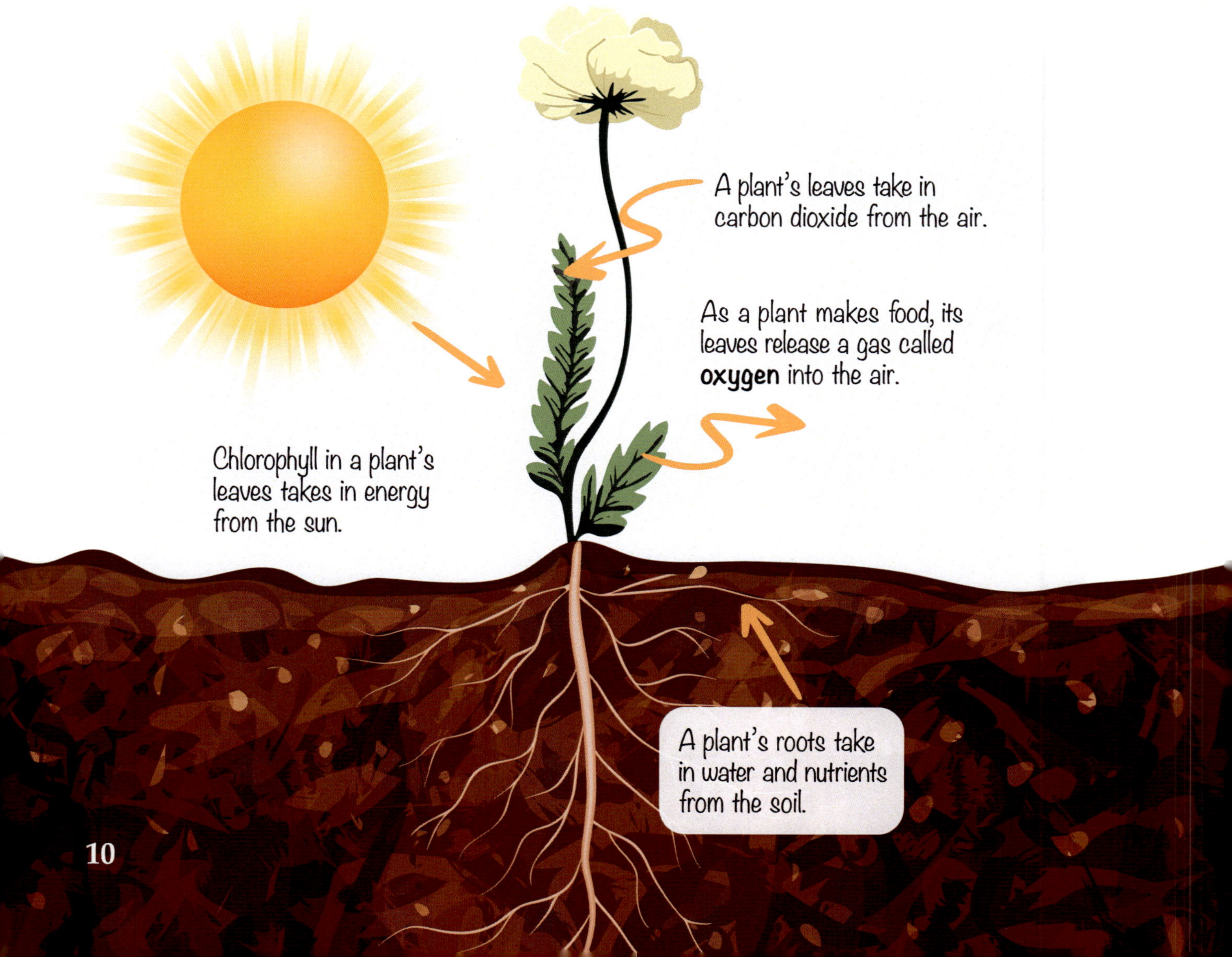

Helping animals

As they make food, plants help many animals stay healthy. Plants use carbon dioxide for photosynthesis. Breathing too much carbon dioxide is harmful to animals. Plants also release oxygen into the air. Animals must breathe oxygen to survive.

TUNDRA PLANTS

In summer, the sun may shine for 24 hours a day on the tundra. This amount of sunlight helps hundreds of colorful plants grow in just a few weeks. Most plants could not survive in the tundra's freezing temperatures and thin soil. Tundra plants have **adapted**, or changed, in ways that help them survive.

Many tundra plants, such as the arctic poppy shown left, have waxy or hairy stems and leaves. Having waxy and hairy stems and leaves helps keep plants from losing water.

Tundra plants grow low to the ground. Short plants are sheltered from the strong winds that blow across the tundra.

Helpful plants

Lichens are important tundra plants. They are eaten by many tundra animals. Orange, yellow, or black lichens often grow on rocks. As lichens grow, they slowly break up the rocks. Over time, the pieces of rock become smaller and smaller. The small rocks eventually form new soil.

Most tundra plants are **perennials**. Perennials are plants that can live for many years by growing only in summer. The dwarf willow herb above is a perennial that grows on the tundra.

Arctic cotton grass has many seeds. The seeds make up the fluff you see in the picture. They are spread by the wind. New plants can grow where the seeds land.

TUNDRA PLANT-EATERS

Musk oxen are grazers that live on the tundra year round. In winter, they use their hooves to dig up grasses buried beneath the snow.

A few herbivores, such as musk oxen and arctic hares, live on the tundra year round. Many other herbivores go to the tundra only in summer. They travel long distances. These animals must eat a lot of tundra plants to get the food energy they need.

Different plant foods

Most tundra herbivores are **grazers**. Grazers are animals that eat grasses and other small plants. Caribou and musk oxen are large tundra grazers. Caribou eat lichens. They scrape the lichens from rocks using their **hooves**. Other tundra herbivores are **browsers**. Browsers eat leaves, shoots, and twigs.

Arctic hares are browsers. They feed on leaves, lichens, berries, and shoots.

Eating plant parts

Different tundra herbivores eat different foods. Arctic ground squirrels and other small animals eat the berries, leaves, seeds, and flowers of plants. Arctic bumblebees and some birds feed on **nectar**. Nectar is a sweet liquid found in flowers.

Many grasshoppers live on the tundra. Grasshoppers eat grasses and clover.

Dall's sheep are tundra herbivores that eat grasses, flowers, and many kinds of arctic **mosses**. Mosses are small green plants that grow in clumps.

TUNDRA ANIMALS

red fox

arctic fox

The ears of the arctic fox are much smaller than are the ears of the red fox. The red fox lives in warmer areas.

Many tundra animals, such as the arctic hare above, have large feet. Large feet help keep arctic animals from sinking into the snow.

A polar bear's coat is made up of hollow hairs. The hairs trap heat and keep the bear warm.

The bodies of animals that live on the tundra year round have adapted to survive the cold. Most tundra animals have small bodies and tiny ears. Having small bodies and ears keeps animals from losing body heat in winter.

On the move

Some animals do not live on the tundra year round. Arctic terns, caribou, and grizzly bears **migrate** to and from the tundra each year. They travel long distances to the tundra from the south each summer to feed on plants. Arctic terns migrate farther than any other animal. They travel to the tundra from the South Pole and back!

Little lemmings

Lemmings are small herbivores that live in groups on the tundra all year. In winter, lemmings build tunnels under the snow. The tunnels lead to small rooms. The lemmings gather grasses and animal fur for each room. The grasses and fur help keep the rooms warm.

Many babies

Lemmings have many babies each year. They sometimes have more babies than they can feed. When lemmings cannot find enough food, they move as a group to look for more food. As the lemmings travel, some of them drown as they cross rivers.

Important to food chains

Lemmings are among the most important animals in tundra food chains. Most tundra carnivores eat lemmings. Without lemmings, tundra carnivores would not have enough food to eat.

TUNDRA MEAT-EATERS

The tundra is home to many carnivores. Some of these carnivores are **predators**. Predators hunt other animals for food. The animals predators hunt are called **prey**. The main predators on the tundra are arctic foxes, arctic wolves, and owls, such as the snowy owl shown left. In summer, polar bears also hunt on the tundra.

Kinds of predators

There are two kinds of predators. Secondary consumers are predators that hunt and eat herbivores. **Tertiary consumers** are predators that hunt and eat other carnivores. "Tertiary" means "third." Tertiary consumers are the third group of animals in a food chain that eat to get energy.

A wolf is a secondary consumer when it eats a herbivore such as a lemming. It is a tertiary consumer when it eats a snowy owl, which is also a carnivore.

Important predators

Predators are important animals in tundra food chains. Without predators, the **populations** of many kinds of herbivores would grow too large. If there were too many herbivores, they would eat all the tundra plants.

The perfect prey

Predators also keep animal populations healthy by hunting young, old, and sick animals. These animals are the easiest for predators to catch. When predators remove weak animals from food chains, there is more food available for the remaining healthy animals.

The arctic fox, shown below, is the most common tundra predator. It feeds mainly on lemmings and arctic hares. Without the arctic fox, the populations of lemmings and arctic hares would soon grow too large.

THE SEARCH FOR FOOD

Tundra predators have different ways of catching prey. The gyrfalcon, shown right, flies low to the ground while chasing prey. It chases its prey until it catches the tired animal. Lynx kittens work with their mothers to hunt arctic hares. To begin the hunt, the lynxes spread out over a large area and hide in different places. When an arctic hare hops by, the lynxes jump out from their hiding places and chase the hare. A lynx catches an arctic hare by striking the hare with its large paws and sharp claws.

Following predators

Carnivores do not always hunt and kill their own prey. Most tundra carnivores are also **scavengers**. Scavengers are animals that feed on **carrion**, or dead animals. Scavengers, such as the wolverine shown above, often follow large tundra predators such as polar bears and wolves. When the predators are through eating the animals they have killed, the scavengers move in and finish the meals.

Cleaning the tundra

Scavengers get energy from the nutrients in carrion. Scavengers keep the tundra clean as they eat by removing the bodies of dead animals.

TUNDRA OMNIVORES

Some tundra animals are **omnivores**. Omnivores eat both plants and animals. Arctic ground squirrels, shown below, are omnivores that eat seeds, fruits, and leaves, as well as carrion and insects.

Many choices

In winter, tundra animals often have trouble finding food. Omnivores have less trouble finding food than do herbivores or carnivores. Omnivores are **opportunistic feeders**. Opportunistic feeders eat any food that they can find.

The ptarmigan, shown above, lives on the tundra all year. It eats plants, seeds, berries, and insects.

Food for grizzlies

Grizzly bears are huge animals that can weigh up to 1,500 pounds (680 kg)! They can run quickly and are big enough to kill other large animals, such as moose. Grizzly bears rarely hunt other animals, however. They eat mainly berries and plants. Although grizzly bears eat plant foods, they are omnivores because they also eat fish and small animals such as lemmings and ground squirrels. When looking for meat to eat, grizzly bears often watch for predators that have just killed an animal. They then chase away the predators and steal their food.

DECOMPOSERS CLEAN UP

Dead plants and animals that are **decomposing**, or breaking down, still contain many nutrients. **Decomposers** are living things that eat **detritus**, or decomposing plants and animals. When decomposers eat detritus, they take in some of the leftover nutrients.

Detritus food chains

When decomposers eat dead plants and animals, they form a **detritus food chain**. Some tundra decomposers include mushrooms, snails, **bacteria**, and molds.

A detritus food chain

When a plant or an animal such as this wolf dies, it becomes dead material in the soil.

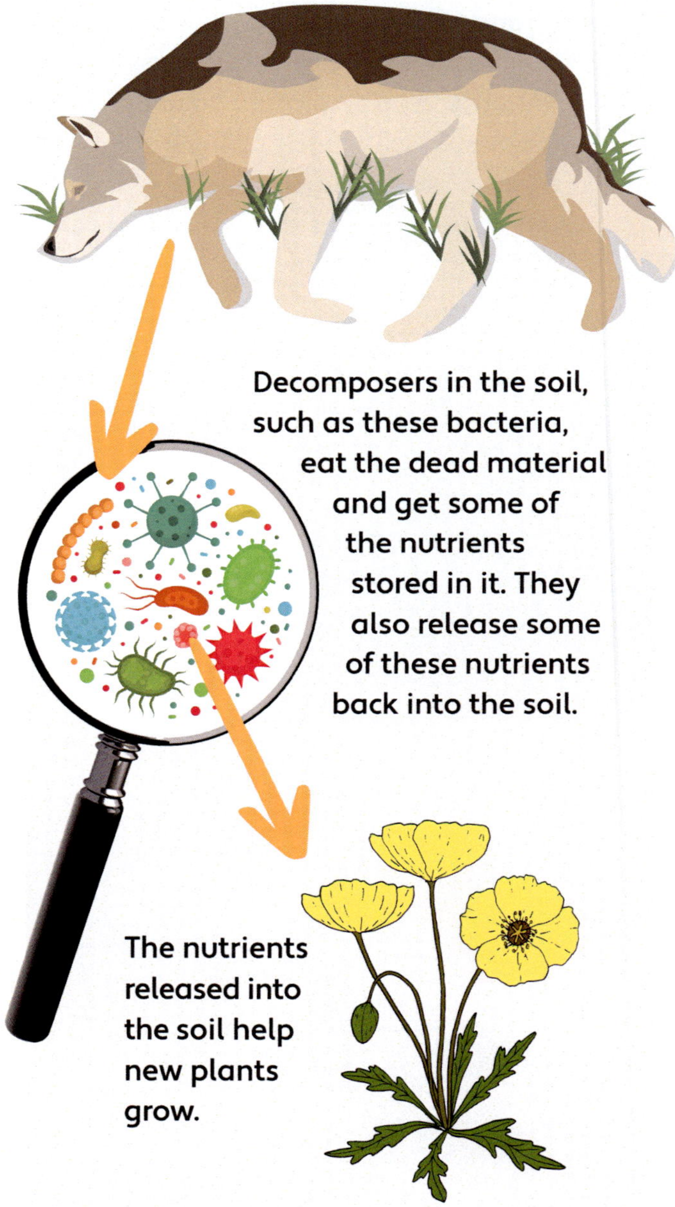

Decomposers in the soil, such as these bacteria, eat the dead material and get some of the nutrients stored in it. They also release some of these nutrients back into the soil.

The nutrients released into the soil help new plants grow.

Note: The arrows point toward the living things that receive nutrients.

Helping food chains

Decomposers help plants and animals at every level of a food chain. Decomposers add nutrients to soil. New plants need nutrients to grow. When many plants grow, herbivores have plenty of food. Herbivores that eat a lot of food stay healthy. Healthy animals can have many babies. When there are many herbivores, the carnivores have plenty of food to eat, as well.

Decomposers are food, too! Many animals, including young ptarmigans, eat snails.

TUNDRA FOOD WEBS

A single food chain contains plants, a herbivore, and a carnivore. When an animal from one food chain eats a plant or an animal from another food chain, the food chains become connected.

Food chains that are connected form a **food web**. There are many food webs on the tundra. Most tundra animals eat different kinds of foods. As a result, these animals belong to many food webs.

Food webs often change with the seasons. In winter, carnivores such as this lynx, hunt animals that live on the tundra all year. Their winter food includes arctic hares. In summer, the lynx will hunt young caribou and other animals that migrate to the tundra for food.

A tundra food web

This diagram shows a tundra food web. The arrows point toward the living things that are receiving energy.

TROUBLE ON THE TUNDRA!

The tundra is an important natural area. Tundra plants and animals are being harmed by the actions of people, however. Large amounts of oil lie thousands of feet below the surface of the tundra. People use oil to run their cars and heat their homes. Oil companies use large drills to reach the oil. Drilling for oil **pollutes** the land.

Scared animals

Oil drills are noisy. They often scare tundra animals. Some drills are built in areas through which caribou migrate as they travel to the tundra. The animals are often too afraid to pass the drills. If they do not reach the tundra, many of the caribou may starve.

These caribou are swimming across a river as they migrate to the tundra.

The ice is melting!

The Arctic is warming up! Scientists have discovered that the ice in this northern area is melting much more quickly than they expected it would. The ice is melting because of **global warming**. Global warming is caused by burning fuels such as oil and gas. People use these fuels in their homes and cars. Warmer temperatures in the Arctic will cause the permafrost on the tundra to melt. When the tundra floods, plants cannot grow. Birds will lose their nesting areas. Herbivores will starve. Without herbivores, carnivores will not have enough food!

Global warming may cause many animals to become **endangered** or even **extinct**. If temperatures continue to rise, polar bears may disappear from Earth because they will not have enough food.

PROTECTING THE TUNDRA

You can help

No matter where you live, you can help save the tundra! There are many things you can do every day to make sure the tundra remains a healthy place for plants and animals.

On your feet!

One of the best ways to help the tundra and the animals that live there is to **conserve** oil. To conserve means to use less. You and your family can use less oil by walking, riding bicycles, or using public transportation instead of using a car.

Lights out!

You can also conserve oil by turning off lights in empty rooms in your home. Also, do not forget to turn off your television sets, computers, and stereos!

Tundra animals need a lot of room in which to roam! By conserving oil, your family can help make sure there will be fewer oil drills on the tundra.

GLOSSARY

Note: Boldfaced words that are defined in the text may not appear in the glossary.

bacteria Tiny living things that break down dead plants and animals

carbon dioxide A gas found in the air that plants need to make food

coniferous Describing trees that have cones and needle-shaped leaves

endangered Describing animals that are in danger of dying out

energy The power living things get from food, which helps them move, grow, and stay healthy

extinct Describing animals that no longer live anywhere on Earth

global warming The rising of the temperature of Earth

hooves Tough coverings on the feet of cattle, horses, and caribou

migrate To move from one area to another for a certain period of time

oxygen A gas that animals need to breathe, and which plants release into the air

pigment A natural color found in plants and animals

pollute To make an area dirty by adding to it garbage or other substances that are harmful to the environment

population The total number of a type of plant or animal living in a certain place

INDEX